MW00423683

A MEASURING SCALE FOR ABILITY IN SPELLING

LEONARD P. AYRES

DIVISION OF EDUCATION
RUSSELL SAGE FOUNDATION
130 EAST TWENTY-SECOND STREET
NEW YORK CITY

E 139   9-16-20

Printing Statement:

Due to the very old age and scarcity of this book,
many of the pages may be hard to read due to the
blurring of the original text, possible missing pages,
missing text, dark backgrounds and other issues
beyond our control.

Because this is such an important and rare work, we
believe it is best to reproduce this book regardless of
its original condition.

Thank you for your understanding.

A MEASURING SCALE FOR ABILITY IN SPELLING

During 1914 and the earlier months of 1915 the Division of Education of the Russell Sage Foundation has been conducting a study of spelling among school children with the object of developing a scale for measuring attainment in the spelling of common words. The object of this report is to describe the investigation and to present the scale which it has produced.

As a first step, it was decided to select a large number of the commonest words and to have them spelled by many school children in order to locate standards of spelling attainment in the several grades. In undertaking this work, it seemed worth while to have the children spell not merely common words, but the commonest words, in order to have the entire study based on what may be termed a foundation spelling vocabulary.

One thousand words were finally selected as constituting such a foundation vocabulary. They were chosen by combining the results of the four most extensive studies that have attempted to identify the words most commonly used in different sorts of English writing.

The first of these studies was published by the Rev. J. Knowles in London, England, in 1904 in a pamphlet entitled, "The London Point System of Reading for the Blind." The author says of it, "Taking passages from the English Bible and from various authors, containing 100,000 words, a list was made of the 353 words which occurred most frequently, and the number of times each occurred was noted."

The second of the studies was made by R. C. Eldridge of Niagara Falls and the results were published in 1911 in a pamphlet entitled, "Six Thousand Common English Words." Mr. Eldridge made an analysis of the vocabularies of 250 different articles taken from four issues of four Sunday newspapers published in Buffalo. He found that they contained a total vocabulary of 6,002 different words, which with their repetitions made an aggregate of 43,989 running words.

He reported the number of times that each word appeared.

The third study was conducted by the present writer in 1913 and the results were published by the Division of Education of the Russell Sage Foundation in a monograph entitled, "The Spelling Vocabularies of Personal and Business Letters." The study consisted of the tabulation of 23,629 words from 2,000 short letters written by 2,000 people. The total vocabulary used was found to consist of 2,001 different words and the number of appearances of each was reported.

The last of these four studies was carried through by W. A. Cook and M. V. O'Shea and the results presented in 1914 in a book entitled, "The Child and His Spelling," published by the Bobbs-Merrill Company. This study consisted of the tabulation of some 200,000 words taken from the family correspondence of 13 adults. The total vocabulary was found to consist of 5,200 different words and the number of times each occurred was reported.

FREQUENT USE OF A FEW WORDS

There is one salient characteristic common to all of these studies. This is the cumulative

7

evidence that a few words do most of our work when we write. In every one of the studies it was found that about nine words recur so frequently that they constitute in the aggregate one-fourth of the whole number of words written, while about 50 words constitute with their repetitions one-half of all the words we write. With the exception of *very*, these words are all monosyllables.

It seems reasonable to argue from such evidence that we should do well to find out from such studies as these which words those are that constitute the foundation vocabulary used in ordinary English writing and teach them in our schools so thoroughly that the children by every day use would permanently master them. It seems equally clear that such a list of words forms a better basis for determining standards of spelling attainment than would one made of less commonly used words. For these reasons it was determined to combine the results of the several studies so as to secure the most reliable available list as a foundation for the work.

At first the purpose was to identify the 2,000 most commonly used words, but this project was abandoned because it was soon found to be impossible of realization. It is

8

easily possible to identify the 10 commonest words in written English. These are probably *the, and, of, to, I, a, in, that, you, for.* With their repetitions they constitute more than one-fourth of all the words we write. Save for the personal pronouns, they are essential in writing about any subject, whatever its nature, from Aaron through zythum. It is likewise possible to identify the 50 commonest words, for, like the first 10, they are true construction words and necessary, no matter what the nature of the subject under consideration. With progressively decreasing reliability the list may be extended to include the 500 commonest words and possibly the 1,000 commonest, but not the 2,000 commonest, for long before this point is reached the identity of the frequently used words varies according to the subject under consideration. For this reason it was decided to limit the foundation vocabulary to 1,000 words.

THE THOUSAND COMMONEST WORDS

The list of 1,000 words finally selected was determined upon by finding the frequency with which each word appeared in the tabulations of each study, weighting that frequency according to the size of the base of which it was a part, adding the four frequencies thus obtained, and finding their average. The resulting figure shows how many times the word was repeated in each 100,000 words of written English. The aggregate amount of written material analyzed in securing these results was approximately 368,000 words, written by some 2,500 different persons. More than two-thirds of the material consisted of personal and business letters.

The tabulation of these frequencies furnished a list of several thousand words which were arranged in the descending order of the frequencies with which they occurred. From this list the 1,000 commonest words were selected and have been used as the basis for the present study. These words, together with the figures showing the frequency of appearance of each, per 100,000 running words, are given in List A beginning on page 12. The figures inserted after each 50 words show the cumulative frequencies from the beginning. Thus the first of these figures shows that the 50 commonest words are repeated so frequently that with their repetitions they constitute nearly half of all the words we write. The first 300 words make up more than three-fourths of all writing of this kind and the 1,000 words with their repetitions constitute more than nine-tenths of this sort of written material.

In making up this list, there has been no attempt to reduce all the words to a dictionary basis. Instead the attempt has been to include all the forms of the words which present different spelling difficulties. Thus the various forms of the verb "be" are included as separate words because they present separate spelling difficulties. In the same way "man" and "men," "woman" and "women," are included for the same reason. On the other hand, plurals and verb forms presenting no characteristic spelling difficulties beyond those inherent in the singular or infinitive have not been included. This procedure has necessitated making many arbitrary decisions, but in each case the controlling purpose has been to make each decision on the basis of spelling difficulty.

While the frequencies appearing in List A have been derived as described, it should be explained that not all of the commonest words of the Cook-O'Shea list appear in this new list. This is because their publication did not appear until the present work was well under way and most of the spelling tests had been concluded. However, careful efforts have been made to include all words appearing so frequently that the evidence seemed to warrant their inclusion. While the present list of commonest words can be improved upon, still it is believed to be more reliable as a foundation spelling vocabulary than any one of the previous lists.

LIST A. THE THOUSAND COMMONEST WORDS ARRANGED IN THE DESCENDING ORDER OF THEIR FREQUENCY. THE FIGURES INDICATE THE NUMBER OF OCCURRENCES PER EACH HUNDRED THOUSAND RUNNING WORDS. THE FIGURES INSERTED AFTER EACH FIFTY WORDS ARE CUMULATIVE FREQUENCIES FROM THE BEGINNING

the	6,393	on	667	would	362
and	3,438	he	619	she	359
of	3,422	by	611	or	348
to	3,217	but	572	there	341
I	2,387	my	557	her	311
a	1,911	this	551	an	298
in	1,904	his	543		49,615
that	1,422	which	540		
you	1,306	dear	523	when	288
for	1,241	from	488	time	279
it	1,197	are	468	go	277
was	991	all	448	some	273
is	931	me	444	any	257
will	873	so	432	can	250
as	854	one	428	what	244
have	846	if	408	send	242
not	831	they	400	out	238
with	822	had	397	them	238
be	816	has	391	him	233
your	793	very	383	more	232
at	698	were	368	about	220
we	695	been	370	no	220

please	211	made	144	get	101
week	211	know	143	into	99
night	206	year	143	let	98
their	205	before	138	yesterday	98
other	203	long	137	come	97
up	201	sincerely	135	ever	97
our	200	shall	133	girl	97
good	198	sent	131	also	96
say	198	us	131	where	96
could	193	give	130	while	96
who	192	Mr.	129	did	95
may	189	like	128	little	95
letter	188	enclose	126	look	94
make	185	next	125	respectfully	94
write	182	want	125	afternoon	93
thing	181	hope	122	Miss	93
think	180	love	121	those	93
should	178	men	121	too	93
truly	178	old	118	man	92
now	177	every	117	own	92
its	175	find	117	receive	91
two	173	most	117	soon	91
take	172	such	117	once	89
thank	170	today	117	street	88
do	169	must	116	ask	87
after	168	way	116	down	87
than	167	first	115	yet	87
sir	163	new	113	see	86
last	161	seem	113	since	86
house	160	morning	112	cannot	85
just	160	school	112	help	85
over	160	great	111	away	83
then	159	wish	110	course	83
work	158	home	109	through	83
day	157	feel	106	call	82
here	157	glad	106	meet	82
	59,591	never	106	people	80
		three	106	another	79
said	153	much	105	number	78
only	151	how	103	place	78
well	151	until	103	Sunday	78
am	147	many	102	use	78
these	146	put	102	church	77
tell	145		65,759	nice	77
even	144			sure	77

anything	76	mean	63	why	52
hour	76	quite	63	perhaps	51
children	75	Saturday	63	answer	50
don't	75	again	62	half	50
four	75	Friday	62	keep	50
	70,122	something	62	life	50
		talk	62	ago	49
kind	75	though	62	business	49
oblige	75	office	61	does	49
nothing	74	Tuesday	61	each	49
off	74	best	60	eight	49
believe	73	came	60	knew	49
boy	73		73,452	picture	49
city	73			show	49
found	72	says	60	build	48
pay	72	car	59	care	48
tomorrow	71	ground	59	eye	48
doctor	70	room	59	gentleman	48
five	70	thought	59	head	48
o'clock	70	under	59		76,111
read	70	board	58		
back	69	far	58	left	48
enough	69	nine	58	whether	48
fine	69	without	58	interest	47
order	69	arrest	57	January	47
bed	68	trip	57	present	47
cold	68	cent	56	teacher	47
live	68	right	56	tire	47
mail	68	side	56	upon	47
few	67	Thursday	56	young	47
hear	66	friend	55	done	46
child	65	bad	54	high	46
mother	65	late	54	sorry	46
return	65	money	54	train	46
same	65	need	54	whom	46
almost	64	still	54	broke	45
because	64	book	53	during	45
big	64	hand	53	feet	45
Monday	64	mile	53	itself	45
month	64	paper	53	several	45
start	64	party	53	brought	44
always	63	word	53	everything	44
both	63	madam	52	run	44
cordially	63	six	52	took	44
expect	63	ten	52	better	43

14

lost	43	seen	39	summer	34
possible	43	whole	39	together	34
September	43	whose	39	against	33
sick	43	action	38	clean	33
visit	43	change	38	decide	33
went	43	court	38	issue	33
act	42	follow	38	Mrs.	33
begin	42	matter	38	near	33
desire	42	cost	37	prompt	33
eat	42	February	37	question	33
guess	42	lady	37	ring	33
hard	42	part	37	sit	33
line	42	reply	37	stamp	33
mind	42	spend	37	turn	33
October	42	attend	36	winter	33
poor	42	case	36	busy	32
remember	42	fall	36	folks	32
Wednesday	42	however	36	happy	32
women	42	July	36	lake	32
wonder	42	report	36	maybe	32
conference	41	speak	36	obtain	32
died	41	vote	36	pass	32
glass	41	wife	36	ran	32
held	41	bring	35	study	32
less	41	company	35	become	31
understand	41	cut	35	December	31
	78,302	member	35	dress	31
		November	35	early	31
along	40	open	35	either	31
August	40	reach	35	end	31
evening	40	regard	35	except	31
father	40	woman	35	farther	31
forenoon	40	according	34	heard	31
large	40		80,175	March	31
meant	40			person	31
seven	40	between	34	rather	31
address	39	bill	34	water	31
charge	39	certain	34	written	31
family	39	copy	34	April	30
finish	39	deal	34	Christmas	30
hot	39	director	34		81,794
known	39	might	34		
least	39	move	34	country	30
plan	39	rain	34	fact	30
saw	39	small	34	herself	30

immediate	30	running	27	arrive	24
marriage	30	separate	27	began	24
May	30			carry	24
provision	30		83,220	distribute	24
reason	30	sold	27	earliest	24
slide	30	told	27	effort	24
story	30	although	26	hat	24
unfortunate	30	among	26	justice	24
arrange	29	association	26	lose	24
awful	29	close	26		
complete	29	club	26		84,479
fire	29	dollar	26	lot	24
forget	29	evidence	26	material	24
gave	29	form	26	nor	24
kill	29	himself	26	sometimes	24
mere	29	intend	26	struck	24
nearly	29	June	26	unable	24
neither	29	list	26	various	24
noon	29	public	26	anyway	23
past	29	station	26	band	23
service	29	table	26	boat	23
unless	29	true	26	dark	23
aunt	28	already	25	difference	23
ball	28	appreciate	25	door	23
character	28	body	25	enter	23
full	28	clear	25	face	23
further	28	cover	25	husband	23
learn	28	driven	25	importance	23
often	28	fair	25	lead	23
principle	28	getting	25	light	23
ride	28	got	25	offer	23
second	28	instead	25	pleasure	23
sister	28	pleasant	25	prepare	23
size	28	price	25	refer	23
state	28	relative	25	represent	23
thus	28	rule	25	rest	23
yes	28	son	25	river	23
afraid	27	song	25	scene	23
annual	27	sudden	25	special	23
automobile	27	throw	25	stand	23
coming	27	war	25	stop	23
date	27	west	25	trust	23
heart	27	world	25	try	23
law	27	accept	24	walk	23
name	27	alone	24	warm	23

weather	23	wait	21	drown	19
condition	22	worth	21	easy	19
different	22	beside	20	escape	19
else	22	bought	20	free	19
especially	22	built	20	gone	19
game	22	buy	20	happen	19
grant	22	carried	20	hurt	19
indeed	22	destroy	20	led	19
liberty	22	direction	20	low	19
necessary	22	fell	20	mention	19
object	22	fourth	20	promise	19
paid	22	grand	20	result	19
plant	22	hold	20	select	19
popular	22	inform	20	serve	19
post	22	lay	20	soap	19
pretty	22	leave	20	suggest	19
	85,621	length	20	teach	19
		loss	20	terrible	19
prison	22	mine	20	therefore	19
road	22	ought	20	uncle	19
section	22	outside	20	absence	18
subject	22	pair	20	article	18
success	22	probably	20	became	18
supply	22		86,658	behind	18
system	22			brother	18
tax	22	ready	20	dead	18
allow	21	real	20	delay	18
amount	21	request	20	drill	18
appoint	21	spring	20	effect	18
expense	21	stay	20	employ	18
felt	21	stole	20		87,610
fifth	21	themselves	20		
fill	21	third	20	entire	18
front	21	top	20	entrance	18
information	21	toward	20	extreme	18
miss	21	watch	20	fix	18
none	21	wrote	20	forty	18
press	21	account	19	general	18
red	21	across	19	objection	18
salary	21	around	19	perfect	18
secure	21	card	19	period	18
set	21	cause	19	rapid	18
tenth	21	death	19	region	18
ticket	21	divide	19	remain	18
usual	21	doubt	19	repair	18

sail	18	trouble	17	black	15
search	18	aboard	16	claim	15
short	18	air	16	common	15
stood	18	appear	16	convenient	15
suppose	18	beautiful	16	convention	15
view	18	burn	16	daughter	15
white	18	capture	16	declare	15
able	17	career	16	estate	15
above	17	check	16	event	15
assure	17	contain	16	factory	15
auto	17	deep	16	favor	15
baby	17	direct	16	God	15
catch	17	dozen	16	illustrate	15
duty	17	east	16	injure	15
education	17	elect	16	lesson	15
extra	17	election	16	minute	15
fail	17	engage	16	news	15
foot	17	express	16	political	15
forward	17	final	16	prove	15
goes	17	finally	16	rate	15
government	17	gold	16	soft	15
impossible	17	horse	16	suffer	15
include	17	motion	16	surprise	15
income	17	north	16	tree	15
increase	17	occupy	16	wear	15
inside	17	preliminary	16	within	15
investigate	17	principal	16	yard	15
judgment	17	proceed	16	age	14
navy	17	provide	16	athletic	14
omit	17	refuse	16	attention	14
opinion	17	relief	16	avenue	14
police	17	retire	16	bear	14
position	17	shed	16	begun	14
power	17	sight	16	belong	14
prefer	17	south	16	camp	14
proper	17	spent	16	cast	14
push	17	stopped	16	circular	14
	88,480	vacation	16	class	14
		weigh	16	clothing	14
raise	17	wind	16	collect	14
really	17	wonderful	16	colonies	14
round	17	add	15	combination	14
shut	17	affair	15	comfort	14
tonight	17	attempt	15	complaint	14
total	17		89,284	consideration	14

18

disappoint	14	emergency	13	associate	12
distinguish	14	empire	13	await	12
due	14	engine	13	beginning	12
feature	14	enjoy	13	block	12
field	14	entertain	13	blow	12
	90,011	entitle	13	blue	12
		estimate	13	born	12
firm	14	experience	13	box	12
human	14	fight	13	bridge	12
manner	14	figure	13	celebration	12
neighbor	14	file	13	center	12
progress	14	flight	13	century	12
recent	14		90,673	chain	12
sea	14			circumstance	12
session	14	flower	13	citizen	12
statement	14	foreign	13	connection	12
suit	14	guest	13	convict	12
theater	14	history	13	develop	12
visitor	14	important	13	examination	12
agréement	13	imprison	13		91,299
alike	13	improvement	13		
allege	13	jail	13	famous	12
application	13	newspaper	13	fortune	12
argument	13	organization	13	height	12
arrangement	13	personal	13	honor	12
beg	13	piece	13	ice	12
chief	13	play	13	inspect	12
cities	13	primary	13	invitation	12
clerk	13	receipt	13	judge	12
command	13	responsible	13	land	12
committee	13	restrain	13	ledge	12
concern	13	royal	13	local	12
consider	13	secretary	13	machine	12
contract	13	spell	13	majority	12
crowd	13	stone	13	mayor	12
dash	13	summon	13	measure	12
debate	13	testimony	13	mountain	12
decision	13	track	13	national	12
degree	13	travel	13	official	12
department	13	victim	13	organize	12
diamond	13	accident	12	page	12
difficulty	13	addition	12	particular	12
discussion	13	adopt	12	point	12
district	13	army	12	population	12
elaborate	13	assist	12	pound	12

practical	12	railroad	12	term	12
president	12	recommend	12	town	12
print	12	recover	12	treasure	12
private	12	reference	12	vessel	12
property	12	senate	12	volume	12
publication	12	serious	12	wire	12
publish	12	ship	12	witness	12
purpose	12	steamer	12	wreck	12
race	12	support	12		91,899

Co-operation of City Superintendents

When the 1,000 words had been selected, letters were written to city superintendents of schools throughout the country asking if they would co-operate in the work by having lists of 20 words each given as spelling tests in all the grades of their school systems from the second through the eighth. Almost without exception they generously agreed to undertake this part of the work, and satisfactory returns were finally secured from the following 84 cities:

Akron, Ohio
Albany, N. Y.
Asbury Park, N. J.
Atlanta, Ga.
Auburn, N. Y.
Augusta, Ga.
Bangor, Me.
Bay City, Mich.
Bayonne, N. J.
Boise, Idaho
Bridgeport, Ct.
Brockton, Mass.
Burlington, Vt.

Cedar Rapids, Iowa
Chicopee, Mass.
Colorado Springs, Colo.
Columbus, Ohio
Covington, Ky.
Cripple Creek, Colo.
Cumberland, Md.
Danville, Ill.
Denver, Colo.
Des Moines, Iowa
Detroit, Mich.
Dubuque, Iowa
Duluth, Minn.

20

East Orange, N. J.
Elizabeth, N. J.
Evanston, Ill.
Evansville, Ind.
Fall River, Mass.
Fitchburg, Mass.
Fort Wayne, Ind.
Galesburg, Ill.
Grand Rapids, Mich.
Greenwich, Ct.
Harrisburg, Pa.
Haverhill, Mass.
Indianapolis, Ind.
Jackson, Mich.
Jersey City, N. J.
Joliet, Ill.
Kalamazoo, Mich.
Kenosha, Wis.
Lawrence, Mass.
Lewiston, Me.
Louisville, Ky.
Manchester, N. H.
Michigan City, Ind.
Middletown, Ct.
Minneapolis, Minn.
Mobile, Ala.
Montclair, N. J.
Muncie, Ind.
Muskegon, Mich.

Nashua, N. H.
New Bedford, Mass.
New Orleans, La.
Newport, Ky.
Newport, R. I.
Newton, Mass.
Oklahoma City, Okla.
Oshkosh, Wis.
Passaic, N. J.
Pittsburg, Pa.
Plainfield, N. J.
Portland, Me.
Raleigh, N. C.
Reading, Pa.
Richmond, Ind.
Richmond, Va.
St. Joseph, Mo.
Schenectady, N. Y.
Somerville, Mass.
South Bend, Ind.
South Manchester, Ct.
Springfield, Mass.
Syracuse, N. Y.
Terre Haute, Ind.
Trenton, N. J.
Utica, N. Y.
Waltham, Mass.
Woonsocket, R. I.
Worcester, Mass.

GIVING THE TESTS

The 1,000 words were first made up into 50 lists of 20 words each and these lists were given as dictated spelling tests. Each list of words was first spelled by the children of two consecutive grades in a number of cities. The work was done at the mid-point of the school year and so arranged in each case as to test the spelling attainment of the children

who had completed just half the work of
each grade. Where words have more than
one meaning for the same pronunciation, the
meaning desired was indicated by giving a
short illustrative sentence.

As a control and check, words were next
taken from each of the 50 lists and recom-
bined in new sets of 20 words each and sent
out as tests in each of four consecutive grades
in the different cities. These two sets of
testing were continued until an aggregate of
1,400,000 spellings had been secured from 70,-
000 children in 84 cities. The results constitute the basis of the present scale.

Problems in Scale Making

To be both valid and convenient, a scale for
measuring attainment in spelling should consist of a series of groups of words so arranged
that all the words in each group are of equal
spelling difficulty, and with the groups so arranged that the step in spelling difficulty from
any one group to the next higher group will be
equal to any other step on the scale from one
group to the next higher group.

In the present work, words have been considered as of equal spelling difficulty if they
are correctly spelled by an equal proportion

of children who have had the same amount of training in spelling, which is to say, by children of the same school grade. It is essential that the words should be of equal difficulty in order to avoid the defect of the ordinary schoolroom test in spelling in which words of greatly varying difficulty are put together in a single 10 or 20 word spelling list, and the pupils' papers marked by taking 10 or 5 points off for each word misspelled. The assumption in such a test is that all the words are equally difficult, whereas this is almost never even approximately true.

The reason why words have been rated as of equal difficulty for given grades in the present study is that it has been found impossible to group them as of equal difficulty for people in general or for school children in general. This is because the easier words are of no difficulty at all for pupils who have had much training, while the same words are of real and varying difficulty for those who have had little training. Similarly, harder words may be of absolute difficulty for children of the lower grades, while they are of varying degrees of difficulty for those of the upper grades. Hence, words can be grouped as of equal difficulty only when we find that they are of equal difficulty for people who have had equal amounts of training; for example, school children of a given grade. Moreover, a valid scale should embrace only words that are normally within the usual writing vocabularies of the children, for otherwise words will be rated as of high degrees of difficulty which are in reality simply unusual. This consideration has been cared for in the present work by confining the entire study to the most commonly used words.

LOCATING THE EQUAL STEPS ON THE SCALE

After the degree of difficulty of each word for pupils of a given grade had been ascertained by finding what per cent of the pupils could spell it correctly, the next problem was to arrange the words in groups which should be of such progressive degrees of difficulty that all the steps in difficulty from one group to the next, to the next, and so on, should be equal steps. It was necessary to insure that the words in the second group should be as much harder than those in the first, as those in the third were harder than those in the second, and so on for all the successive groups of the scale. The final purpose was to locate these

24

groups at equally spaced steps on a scale from 0 to 100.

The method employed in locating the equal steps on the scale was based on the assumption that spelling ability conforms in general to what is known as the normal distribution.

Spelling Ability and the Normal Distribution

This assumption is based on the well known principle that intellectual abilities are distributed in much the same way among people as are physical traits. Just as there are in a normal population very few dwarfs, many people of about medium height, and very few giants, so there are very few exceedingly poor spellers, many medium ones, and very few truly excellent ones. That this assumption was valid in the present case will be shown later.

The so-called normal curve illustrating such a distribution is reproduced in Diagram 1. The properties of the normal curve have been most accurately determined. Let us suppose that this represents the distribution of spelling ability among a large number of third grade children.

The area enclosed between the curve and

25

the base line represents all the children ranged according to spelling ability. At the extreme left the curve is very near the base which indicates the small number of very poor spellers.

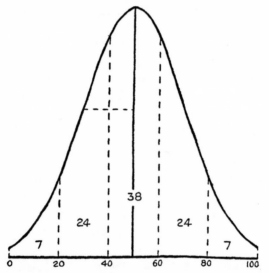

Diagram 1.—Surface of normal distribution with base line five times the sigma distance in length and divided as a scale running from 0 to 100

In the middle the curve is distant from the base representing the large proportion of medium spellers. At the right the curve is again very near the base representing the

26

small proportion of excellent spellers. The median line at the 50 per cent point represents the average ability.

The dotted horizontal line from the median to the curve represents the sigma distance and intersects the curve at the point at which it changes from convex to concave. This distance is always a constant function of the curve of normal distribution and in the present study has been chosen as the basis of the measurements along the base line. If we lay out on the base a distance equal to this sigma distance and in such a way that it shall extend equally to the left and right of the 50 per cent point where the median bisects the base, its left end will reach the point marked 40 and its right the one marked 60. If now we lay out the same sigma distance two more times to the left, we shall have the points marked 20 and 0, and by doing the same on the right, we shall have the points marked 80 and 100.

In thus dividing the base into five equal parts, each equal to the sigma distance, and calling the extremes 0 and 100, we are taking liberties with the curve of normal distribution for the base and the curves do not actually meet at these points. In theory the two lines are in asymptote and could be indefinitely ex-

MEASURING SCALE FOR ABILITY IN SPELLING

Grade	A	B	C	D	E	F	G	H	I	J	K	L	M	N	O	P	Q	R	S	T	U	V	W	X	Y	Z
2ND	99	98	96	96	94	92	88	84	79	73	66	58	50													
3RD			100	99	98	96	94	92	88	84	79	73	66	58	50											
4TH					100	99	98	96	94	92	88	84	79	73	66	58	50									
5TH							100	99	98	96	94	92	88	84	79	73	66	58	50							
6TH									100	99	98	96	94	92	88	84	79	73	66	58	50					
7TH											100	99	98	96	94	92	88	84	79	73	66	58	50			
8TH													100	99	98	96	94	92	88	84	79	73	66	58	50	

Diagram 2.—Heading of the scale as finally arranged. This reproduction is one-fourth the length of the actual scale, which is 21 inches long. The words as arranged in List C are printed in the 26 columns from A to Z.

tended, always getting nearer together but never touching. In theory about 99.4 per cent of all the cases lie to the right of the point indicated as 0 and some six-tenths of one per cent of them lie to the left. For the purpose of the present study, it has been considered sufficiently accurate to call the point 0 and to assume that all the cases lie to the right. A corresponding assumption is made with respect to the 100 point at the right end of the line.

On the basis of these assumptions, we find that the area of the curve beginning at the left and extending as far as the vertical line at the point 20 is seven per cent of the total. Between this line and the one at point 40 are 24 per cent of the cases, making a total to this point of 31 per cent. From here to point 60 are 38 per cent, making a total from the beginning of 69 per cent. From this point to point 80 are 24 per cent of the cases, making a total of 93 per cent, and from here to 100 are the remaining seven cases.

SCALING THE WORDS

Now we find that among third grade children in general seven in each 100 fail in the attempt to spell the word *has*, while 93 spell it correctly. Thus if we imagine the normal curve of Diagram 1 as representing 100 typical third grade children ranked according to spelling ability with the worst at the left and the rest in order of ability to the right, we should find that the line at point 20 would fall at such a place that the seven in the 100 who fail on *has* would be to the left of the line while the 93 who can spell it would be on the right. In a similar way the line at 40 would leave on the left the 31 children who fail on *almost* and on its right the 69 who spell it correctly. By this same method all of the words have been located according to their location on a line representing the distance in spelling difficulty from the word so easy that just all can spell it correctly to the one at the other extreme so difficult that none can quite spell it correctly. This is the line from 0 to 100 difficulty and the words have all been located on it according to equal steps of distance.

In order to do this, each of the five divisions shown on the base line of Diagram 1 has been subdivided into five equal parts, making a total of 25 steps for the entire scale from 0 to 100. The average of all the values that might theoretically be contained in each of these 25 steps has thus been determined to the nearest whole number and this value has been assigned to the step. These 25 values are 100, 99, 98, 96, 94, 92, 88, 84, 79, 73, 66, 58, 50, 42, 34, 27, 21, 16, 12, 8, 6, 4, 2, 1, 0. They have been used to identify the 25 steps and they indicate the average per cent of correct spellings found among the children of the grade in question, in their spelling of the words placed on the scale at that step. For example, the nine words, *the, in, so, no, now, man, ten, bed, top*, are shown on the scale as at step 94 for the second grade. This indicates that the average per cent correct among second grade attempts to spell these words was 94.

Combining the Scales for the Seven Grades

Since the first data returned by the co-operating school systems consisted of figures showing the number of children succeeding and failing in spelling the words in each of two consecutive grades, it was possible to compute the amount of improvement in spelling the same words from grade to grade. It was possible, that is, to find how much better the third grade children spelled the words than the second grade ones, how much better

31

records the fourth grade pupils made than did the third grade ones in spelling the same words, and so on for all the grades.

When these figures, showing average improvement from grade to grade, were reduced to terms of the 25-division spelling scale that has been described on page 30, it was found that the improvement of the third grade over the second averaged about three steps; that of the fourth over the third averaged about three steps; and the improvement of each of the other five grades over its preceding grade averaged about two steps.

These computations of the average shift in spelling ability were then checked up by combining with them the data for the sets of words spelled in four consecutive grades and the results remained nearly unchanged. A further check was then made by computing the shift found from grade to grade by Dr. B. R. Buckingham in his study entitled, "Spelling Ability," published in 1913 by Teachers College, Columbia University. A fourth´ check was made by comparing with these results those reported by Dr. Buckingham for the use of Dr. J. M. Rice's spelling test. The results of the three investigations all reduced to terms of the 25-step scale of the present study showed average grade shifts as follows:

Grade	Ayres	Bucking-ham	Rice
2nd to 3rd	2.9	3.2	..
3rd to 4th	2.9	2.9	..
4th to 5th	1.9	1.9	2.1
5th to 6th	2.2	2.2	1.8
6th to 7th	1.9	1.6	1.9
7th to 8th	2.0	2.1	2.1
Total	13.8	13.9	

In view of the supporting evidence offered by these several checks, it was decided to adopt, for combining the several scales into one, shifts in advancing spelling ability from grade to grade as follows: second to third, three steps; third to fourth, three steps; fourth to fifth, two steps; fifth to sixth, two steps; sixth to seventh, two steps; seventh to eighth, two steps.

On this basis the scales for the seven grades were put together, one below the other as illustrated on page 28, so that the third grade scale extends three steps beyond the second grade one; the fourth grade scale is three steps beyond the third grade one; and each of the other scales is located two steps beyond its predecessor.

When the headings representing the seven grade scales were thus superimposed on each other with the appropriate shifts from grade to grade, the 1,000 words were entered in the columns below. Their theoretical spelling difficulty in each grade according to the scales was then compared with their difficulties as indicated by the tests in the 84 cities. The results showed that the conformity was so close that if as many as 10 words in one column were considered as a group, the agreement was nearly exact; that among the individual words the very great majority had classroom records in agreement with their scale locations; and that the words spelled in the classrooms by the greatest numbers of children conformed most exactly. These bits of evidence all point in one direction and that is toward the substantiation of the hypothesis that spelling ability among homogeneous groups of school children approximately conforms to the normal distribution. If it followed some radically differing type of distribution, the several scales could not fit together as they do.

34

In its final arrangement, the scale consists of the seven grade scales so superimposed upon each other as to indicate the approximate shifts from grade to grade and with the 1,000 words entered in 26 columns below. This is shown by the illustration on page 28, which reproduces in miniature the heading of the scale and indicates the columns in which the words are printed in the scale itself. The scale as printed for convenient classroom use is a sheet of paper measuring some 14 by 24 inches with the heading as illustrated on page 28 printed across the top, the 1,000 words entered in the appropriate columns, and the directions for use printed in the lower left hand corner.

In order to facilitate identification and reference, the 26 columns of the scale are designated by the letters from A to Z. The 1,000 words are listed in these columns. In order to complete the record and description as presented in this monograph, these words are published here in Lists B and C beginning on pages 43 and 51 respectively. In List B, the 1,000 words are presented in alphabetic order and beside each is the letter indicating the

column in which that word is found on the
scale. In List C, the words are presented in
columns from A through Z, just as they are
published in the scale in its final form.

All the words in each column of the scale
are of approximately equal spelling difficulty.
The steps in spelling difficulty from each column to the next are approximately equal
steps. The numbers at the top of each column on the scale indicate about what per cent
of correct spellings of the words in that column
may be expected among the children of the
different grades. For example, reference to
the scale headings as reproduced on page 28
and the words of column H as printed beginning on page 51 will show that if 20 words
from this column are given as a spelling test,
it may be expected that the average score for
an entire second grade spelling them will be
about 79 per cent. This will be more clearly
understood by referring to the scale as printed
on the large sheet for classroom use. The
average score for an entire third grade taking
the same tests should be about 92 per cent,
for a fourth grade about 98 per cent, and for
a fifth grade about 100 per cent.

The limits of the groups are as follows: 50
means from 46 through 54 per cent; 58 means

from 55 through 62 per cent; 66 means from
63 through 69 per cent; 73 means from 70
through 76 per cent; 79 means from 77
through 81 per cent; 84 means from 82
through 86 per cent; 88 means from 87 through
90 per cent; 92 means from 91 through 93
per cent; 94 means 94 and 95 per cent; 96
means 96 and 97 per cent; while 98, 99, and
100 per cent are separate groups.

By means of these groupings, a child's
spelling ability may be located in terms of
grades. Thus, if a child were given a 20
word spelling test from the words of column
0 and spelled 15 words, or 75 per cent of them,
correctly, it would be proper to say that he
showed fourth grade spelling ability. If he
spelled correctly 17 words, or 85 per cent, he
would show fifth grade ability, and so on.

All of the scales have been arbitrarily cut
off at 50 per cent, partly because it is doubtful
whether any useful teaching purpose is served
by testing children on words of which they
cannot spell more than 50 per cent correctly,
and partly because children of the lower
grades attempting to spell difficult words frequently fail, not because of the inherent difficulty of the spelling, but because the word
form is not yet definitely a part of the chil-

dren's regular vocabulary. Thus the record in spelling these words becomes unreliable and it was considered wisest to omit from the scale the numbers showing the scores which children spelling such words would make.

LENGTH OF WORDS AND SPELLING DIFFICULTY

A mere inspection of the scale shows that practically all of the easier words in the first columns are monosyllables. In the middle of the scale are many words of medium difficulty and medium length. At the right hand are found words of greater difficulty and greater length. Thus it is clear that there is a considerable positive correlation between length and difficulty. If we consider the respective difficulties of the words in the 26 columns as being represented by consecutive numbers running from 1 to 26 and compute the correlation between these difficulties and the lengths of the words in these columns, we get a Pearson coefficient of correlation of .73. This close relationship between the length of the words and their difficulty is probably to be accounted for in part by the fact that mere length tends to increase spelling difficulty and

38

in addition, the longer the word is, the more opportunities it presents for difficult combinations of letters and difficulties arising through inaccurate pronunciation. The correlation between the spelling difficulties and the lengths of the words, computed by the Spearman method, gives a coefficient of .88, while the percentage of unlike signed pairs gives a coefficient of .77 and Galton's graphic method one of .78.

Use and Limitations

The scale that has been produced by this study should be found useful in three ways. In the first place, it consists of a list of 1,000 words which probably constitute a most valuable foundation spelling vocabulary.

In the second place, these words are presented in the final scale in groups of approximately equal spelling difficulty. These groups, which are also printed as List C of the present publication, furnish more reliable material for spelling tests than has heretofore been available. This is because the words of each list are of nearly equal difficulty and hence in using them in spelling tests all of the units of the test are of nearly equal value.

In the third place, the scale is so arranged as to indicate about what percentage of children in the several grades in cities throughout the country succeed in spelling the words correctly. By means of these standards children of the different grades in any locality may be tested as to their spelling attainment and the results compared with those which are found in the corresponding grades in city systems in general. When such tests are made of the spelling attainment of large numbers of children in the different grades in any one locality, the results may be compared with considerable reliability with those here presented for the 84 cities which co-operated in the present study. With less reliability the attainment of a smaller number of grades or of one grade may be tested. With still less reliability the attainment of a single child may be compared with these average results.

In all such testing it must be remembered that the present scale or any scale for measuring spelling attainment will become increasingly and rapidly less reliable for measuring purposes as the children become more accustomed to spelling these particular words. In proportion as these lists are used for the purposes of classroom drill, the scale will become

40

untrustworthy as a measuring instrument. Probably the scale will have served its greatest usefulness in any locality when the school children have mastered these 1,000 words so thoroughly that the scale has become quite useless as a measuring instrument.

LIST B. THE THOUSAND WORDS ARRANGED IN ALPHABETIC ORDER. THE LETTERS INDICATE THE COLUMNS IN WHICH THE WORDS ARE LOCATED IN THE FINAL SCALE

a	C	already	R	assure	U		
able	L	also	M	at	B		
aboard	O	although	Q	athletic	W		
about	H	always	N	attempt	Q		
above	L	am	E	attend	O		
absence	T	among	N	attention	R		
accept	T	amount	P	August	O		
accident	T	an	E	aunt	N		
according	R	and	B	auto	P		
account	M	annual	X	automobile	T		
across	K	another	L	avenue	R		
act	N	answer	P	await	Q		
action	Q	any	K	away	I		
add	I	anything	L	awful	P		
addition	Q	anyway	M	baby	H		
address	O	appear	O	back	I		
adopt	R	application	U	bad	E		
affair	S	appoint	Q	ball	H		
afraid	O	appreciate	W	band	J		
after	I	April	N	be	F		
afternoon	K	are	G	bear	K		
again	M	argument	T	beautiful	P		
against	R	army	M	became	K		
age	J	around	K	because	L		
ago	E	arrange	Q	become	K		
agreement	U	arrangement	V	bed	D		
air	J	arrest	Q	been	N		
alike	I	arrive	S	before	L		
all	F	article	R	beg	P		
allege	Z	as	H	began	L		
allow	Q	ask	H	begin	M		
almost	M	assist	S	beginning	U		
alone	L	associate	T	begun	M		
along	J	association	V	behind	K		

43

believe	S	carry	N	complete	R
belong	H	case	M	concern	T
beside	M	cast	J	condition	S
best	I	catch	L	conference	T
better	K	cause	N	connection	Q
between	O	celebration	T	consider	R
big	G	cent	K	consideration	U
bill	J	center	N	contain	O
black	L	century	S	contract	M
block	I	certain	S	convenient	X
blow	I	chain	N	convention	R
blue	J	change	M	convict	Q
board	O	character	W	copy	N
boat	J	charge	M	cordially	W
body	L	check	N	cost	K
book	F	chief·	O	could	K
born	M	child	G	country	L
both	M	children	M	course·	S
bought	M	Christmas	R	court	N
box	H	church	L	cover	J
boy	F	circular	T	crowd	Q
bridge	N	circumstance '	U	cut	I
bring	H	cities	P	dark	J
broke	N	citizen '	U	dash	L
brother	K	city	K	date	L
brought	M	claim	Q	daughter	P
build	M	class	K	day	H
built	N	clean	K	dead	L
burn	K	clear	K	deal	M
business	T	clerk	P	dear	I
busy	R	close	L	death	N
but	F	clothing	L	debate	Q
buy	L	club	K	December	N
by	G	cold	G	decide	T
call	H	collect	M	decision	Y
came	I	colonies	U	declare	Q
camp	K	combination	R	deep	J
can	C	come	G	degree	P
cannot	J	comfort	O	delay	K
capture	N	coming	K	department	P
car	J	command	Q	desire	P
card	J	committee	X	destroy	P
care	K	common	R	develop	U
career	V	company	O	diamond	R
carried	P	complaint	P	did	F

44

died	M	emergency	W	favor	P		
difference	S	empire	P	feature	R		
different	R	employ	Q	February	W		
difficulty	U	enclose	Q	feel	N		
direct	O	end	I	feet	I		
direction	Q	engage	Q	fell	L		
director	R	engine	P	felt	K		
disappoint	X	enjoy	P	few	M		
discussion	V	enough	O	field	Q		
distinguish	U	enter	M	fifth	N		
distribute	R	entertain	R	fight	L		
district	O	entire	Q	figure	O		
divide	U	entitle	T	file	M		
do	A	entrance	P	fill	J		
doctor	N	escape	P	final	Q		
does	P	especially	X	finally	U		
dollar	N	estate	Q	find	I		
done	L	estimate	T	fine	J		
don't	O	even	K	finish	K		
door	H	evening	N	fire	J		
doubt	S	event	M	firm	Q		
down	J	ever	L	first	K		
dozen	N	every	J	five	H		
dress	M	everything	O	fix	M		
drill	M	evidence	V	flight	P		
driven	M	examination	S	flower	L		
drown	R	except	N	folks	T		
due	Q	expect	N	follow	M		
during	O	expense	U	foot	I		
duty	O	experience	V	for	H		
each	I	express	L	foreign	U		
earliest	U	extra	M	forenoon	R		
early	L	extreme	W	forget	J		
east	J	eye	K	form	I		
easy	K	face	I	fortune	P		
eat	H	fact	O	forty	O		
education	R	factory	Q	forward	Q		
effect	R	fail	K	found	J		
effort	Q	fair	N	four	L		
eight	O	fall	I	fourth	O		
either	Q	family	P	free	I		
elaborate	U	famous	Q	Friday	K		
elect	O	far	I	friend	O		
election	P	farther	O	from	J		
else	N	father	L	front	N		

45

full	K	herself	L	is	C		
further	S	high	L	issue	U		
game	J	him	F	it	C		
gave	I	himself	N	its	I		
general	R	his	H	itself	N		
gentleman	Q	history	N	jail	O		
get	H	hold	M	January	N		
getting	O	home	H	judge	O		
girl	J	honor	R	judgment	Z		
give	I	hope	J	July	K		
glad	J	horse	K	June	L		
glass	K	hot	G	just	H		
go	B	hour	K	justice	Q		
God	N	house	H	keep	K		
goes	M	how	H	kill	G		
gold	J	however	L	kind	J		
gone	L	human	P	knew	O		
good	E	hurt	K	know	L		
got	I	husband	P	known	P		
government	S	I	H	lady	K		
grand	J	ice	G	lake	I		
grant	L	if	H	land	G		
great	M	illustrate	R	large	J		
ground	L	immediate	X	last	E		
guess	T	importance	P	late	G		
guest	P	important	Q	law	H		
had	G	impossible	T	lay	H		
half	L	imprison	Q	lead	L		
hand	G	improvement	S	learn	N		
happen	M	in	D	least	N		
happy	J	include	Q	leave	L		
hard	J	income	M	led	H		
has	H	increase	R	ledge	Q		
hat	G	indeed	L	left	J		
have	G	inform	M	length	P		
he	E	information	Q	less	M		
head	K	injure	R	lesson	L		
hear	N	inside	J	let	G		
heard	N	inspect	N	letter	I		
heart	M	instead	O	liberty	O		
height	V	intend	O	life	J		
held	L	interest	R	light	K		
help	J	into	F	like	F		
her	H	investigate	S	line	J		
here	J	invitation	T	list	L		

46

little	E	money	M	occupy	U
live	G	month	M	o'clock	P
local	S	more	J	October	N
long	H	morning	L	of	F
look	F	most	J	off	M
lose	R	mother	G	offer	N
loss	P	motion	S	office	M
lost	J	mountain	M	official	T
lot	H	move	K	often	S
love	H	Mr.	I	old	E
low	H	Mrs.	P	omit	M
machine	R	much	H	on	B
madam	O	must	G	once	L
made	J	my	E	one	H
mail	K	name	J	only	K
majority	U	national	T	open	K
make	G	navy	O	opinion	S
man	D	near	J	or	I
manner	R	nearly	P	order	L
many	L	necessary	U	organization	W
March	L	need	N	organize	T
marriage	S	neighbor	R	other	H
material	U	neither	S	ought	T
matter	N	never	J	our	J
May	J	new	I	out	F
may	F	news	L	outside	J
maybe	K	newspaper	P	over	G
mayor	P	next	L	own	L
me	A	nice	I	page	I
mean	N	night	K	paid	M
meant	U	nine	I	pair	N
measure	Q	no	D	paper	I
meet	L	none	O	part	J
member	M	noon	J	particular	S
men	H	nor	N	party	K
mention	S	north	I	pass	K
mere	U	not	E	past	M
might	M	nothing	L	pay	J
mile	K	November	N	people	L
mind	L	now	D	perfect	O
mine	J	number	N	perhaps	Q
minute	T	object	R	period	Q
Miss	M	objection	O	person	N
miss	I	oblige	P	personal	O
Monday	I	obtain	P	picture	M

47

try	K	warm	L	wind	J
Tuesday	O	was	H	winter	I
turn	L	watch	L	wire	M
two	K	water	K	wish	L
unable	M	way	H	with	J
uncle	O	we	E	within	L
under	J	wear	R	without	K
understand	M	weather	O	witness	S
unfortunate	U	Wednesday	T	woman	N
unless	L	week	K	women	Q
until	O	weigh	R	wonder	N
up	E	well	H	wonderful	Q
upon	K	went	I	word	J
us	E	were	L	work	J
use	N	west	I	world	L
usual	P	what	I	worth	O
vacation	P	when	J	would	K
various	T	where	K	wreck	R
very	I	whether	U	write	N
vessel	R	which	P	written	Q
victim	T	while	M	wrote	N
view	P	white	I	yard	H
visit	P	who	M	year	H
visitor	R	whole	O	yes	H
volume	T	whom	Q	yesterday	N
vote	N	whose	Q	yet	I
wait	P	why	J	you	E
walk	L	wife	K	young	N
want	J	will	E	your	F
war	L				

A
me
do

B
and
go
at
on

C
a
it
is
she
can
see
run

D
the
in
so
no
now
man
ten
bed
top

E
he
you
will
we

an
my
up
last
not
us
am
good
little
ago
old
bad
red

F
of
be
but
this
all
your
out
time
may
into
him
today
look
did
like
six
boy
book

G
by
have

are
had
over
must
make
school
street
say
come
hand
ring
live
kill
late
let
big
mother
three
land
cold
hot
hat
child
ice
play
sea

H
day
eat
sit
lot
box
belong
door
yes
low
soft

stand
yard
bring
tell
five
ball
law
ask
just
way
get
home
much
call
long
love
then
house
year
to
I
as
send
one
has
some
if
how
her
them
other
baby
well
about
men
for
ran
was
that

51

his
led
lay

I

nine
face
miss
ride
tree
sick
got
north
white
spent
foot
blow
block
spring
river
plant
cut
song
winter
stone
free
lake
page
nice
end
fall
feet
went
back
away
paper
put
each
soon
came
Sunday
show
Monday
yet
find

give
new
letter
take
Mr.
after
thing
what
than
its
very
or
thank
dear
west
sold
told
best
form
far
gave
alike
add

J

seven
forget
happy
noon
think
sister
cast
card
south
deep
inside
blue
post
town
stay
grand
outside
dark
band
game

boat
rest
east
son
help
hard
race
cover
fire
age
gold
read
fine
cannot
May
line
left
ship
train
saw
pay
large
near
down
why
bill
want
girl
part
still
place
report
never
found
side
kind
life
here
car
word
every
under
most
made
said

work
our
more
when
from
wind
print
air
fill
along
lost
name
room
hope
same
glad
with
mine

K

became
brother
rain
keep
start
mail
eye
glass
party
upon
two
they
would
any
could
should
city
only
where
week
first
sent
mile
seem
even

without
afternoon
Friday
hour
wife
state
July
head
story
open
short
lady
reach
better
water
round
cost
price
become
class
horse
care
try
move
delay
pound
behind
around
burn
camp
bear
clear
clean
spell
poor
finish
hurt
maybe
across
tonight
tenth
sir
these
club
seen

felt
full
fail
set
stamp
light
coming
cent
night
pass
shut
easy

L

catch
black
warm
unless
clothing
began
able
gone
suit
track
watch
dash
fell
fight
buy
stop
walk
grant
soap
news
small
war
summer
above
express
turn
lesson
half
father
anything
table

high
talk
June
right
date
road
March
next
indeed
four
herself
power
wish
because
world
country
meet
another
trip
list
people
ever
held
church
once
own
before
know
were
dead
leave
early
close
flower
nothing
ground
lead
such
many
morning
however
mind
shall
alone
order

third
push
point
within
done
body

M

trust
extra
dress
beside
teach
happen
begun
collect
file
provide
sight
stood
fix
born
goes
hold
drill
army
pretty
stole
income
bought
paid
enter
railroad
unable
ticket
account
driven
real
recover
mountain
steamer
speak
past
might
begin

53

contract
deal
almost
brought
less
event
off
true
took
again
inform
both
heart
month
children
build
understand
follow
charge
says
member
case
while
also
return
those
office
great
Miss
who
died
change
wire
few
please
picture
money
ready
omit
anyway

N

except
aunt
capture

wrote
else
bridge
offer
suffer
built
center
front
rule
carry
chain
death
learn
wonder
tire
pair
check
prove
heard
inspect
itself
always
something
write
expect
need
thus
woman
young
fair
dollar
evening
plan
broke
feel
sure
least
sorry
press
God
teacher
November
subject
April
history

cause
study
himself
matter
use
thought
person
nor
January
mean
vote
court
copy
act
been
yesterday
among
question
doctor
hear
size
December
dozen
there
tax
number
October
reason
fifth

O

eight
afraid
uncle
rather
comfort
elect
aboard
jail
shed
retire
refuse
district
restrain
royal

objection
pleasure
navy
fourth
population
proper
judge
weather
worth
contain
figure
sudden
forty
instead
throw
personal
everything
rate
chief
perfect
second
slide
farther
duty
intend
company
quite
none
knew
remain
direct
appear
liberty
enough
fact
board
September
station
attend
between
public
friend
during
through
police

until
madam
truly
whole
address
request
raise
August
Tuesday
struck
getting
don't
Thursday

P

spend
enjoy
awful
usual
complaint
auto
vacation
beautiful
flight
travel
rapid
repair
trouble
entrance
importance
carried
loss
fortune
empire
mayor
wait
beg
degree
prison
engine
visit
guest
department
obtain
family

favor
Mrs.
husband
amount
human
view
election
clerk
though
o'clock
support
does
regard
escape
since
which
length
destroy
newspaper
daughter
answer
reply
oblige
sail
cities
known
several
desire
nearly

Q

sometimes
declare
engage
final
terrible
surprise
period
addition
employ
property
select
connection
firm
region

convict
private
command
debate
crowd
factory
publish
represent
term
section
relative
progress
entire
president
measure
famous
serve
estate
remember
either
effort
important
due
include
running
allow
position
field
ledge
claim
primary
result
Saturday
appoint
information
whom
arrest
themselves
special
women
present
action
justice
gentleman
enclose

await
suppose
wonderful
direction
forward
although
prompt
attempt
whose
statement
perhaps
their
imprison
written
arrange

R

forenoon
lose
combination
avenue
neighbor
weigh
wear
entertain
salary
visitor
publication
machine
toward
success
drown
adopt
secure
honor
promise
wreck
prepare
vessel
busy
prefer
illustrate
different
object
provision

55

according
already
attention
education
director
purpose
common
diamond
together
convention
increase
manner
feature
article
service
injure
effect
distribute
general
tomorrow
consider
against
complete
search
treasure
popular
Christmas
interest

S

often
stopped
motion
theater
improvement
century
total
mention
arrive
supply
assist
difference
examination
particular
affair

course
neither
local
marriage
further
serious
doubt
condition
government
opinion
believe
system
possible
piece
certain
witness
investigate
therefore
too
pleasant

T

guess
circular
argument
volume
organize
summon
official
victim
estimate
accident
invitation
accept
impossible
concern
associate
automobile
various
decide
entitle
political
national
recent
business

refer
minute
ought
absence
conference
Wednesday
really
celebration
folks

U

meant
earliest
whether
distinguish
consideration
colonies
assure
relief
occupy
probably
foreign
expense
responsible
beginning
application
difficulty
scene
finally
develop
circumstance
issue
material
suggest
mere
senate
receive
respectfully
agreement
unfortunate
majority
elaborate
citizen
necessary
divide

V

principal
testimony
discussion
arrangement
reference
evidence
experience
session
secretary
association
career
height

W

organization
emergency
appreciate
sincerely
athletic
extreme
practical
proceed
cordially
character
separate
February

X

immediate
convenient
receipt
preliminary
disappoint
especially
annual
committee

Y

decision
principle

Z

judgment
recommend
allege

PUBLICATIONS OF THE DIVISION OF EDUCATION

No. E 61. The Relation of Physical Defects to School Progress. 9 pp. Price, 5 cts.

No. E 94. Measurements as Applied to School Hygiene. 7 pp. Price, 5 cts.

No. E 96. The New Attitude of the School Towards the Health of the Child. 8 pp. Price, 5 cts.

No. E 107. The Binet-Simon Measuring Scale for Intelligence: Some Criticisms and Suggestions. 12 pp. Price, 5 cts.

No. E 108. The Identification of the Misfit Child. 11 pp. Price, 5 cts.

No. E 110. The Relative Responsibility of School and Society for The Over-Age Child. 6 pp. Price, 5 cts.

No. E 111. The Money Cost of Repetition Versus the Money Saving Through Acceleration. 12 pp. Price, 5 cts.

No. E 112. The Relation Between Entering Age and Subsequent Progress Among School Children. 9 pp. Price, 5 cts.

No. E 113. A Scale for Measuring the Quality of Handwriting of School Children. 16 pp. Report, 5 cts. Scale, 5 cts.

No. E 128. Psychological Tests in Vocational Guidance. 6 pp. Price, 5 cts.

57

No. E 130. The Effect of Promotion Rates on School Efficiency. 12 pp. Price, 5 cts.

No. E 132. Fire Protection in Public Schools. 16 pp. Price, 10 cts.

No. E 134. Open Air Schools. 16 pp. Price, 10 cts.

No. E 135. Some Conditions Affecting Problems of Industrial Education in 78 American School Systems. 24 pp. Price, 10 cts.

No. E 136. Constant and Variable Occupations and Their Bearing on Problems of Vocational Education. 12 pp. Price, 5 cts.

No. E 137. A Survey of the Public Schools of Springfield, Illinois. 160 pp. Price, 25 cts.

No. E 138. A Scale for Measuring the Quality of Handwriting of Adults. 11 pp. Report, 5 cts. Scale, 5 cts.

No. E 139. A Measuring Scale for Ability in Spelling. 58 pp. Report, bound in cloth, 30 cts. Scale, 5 cts.

Bulletin E. The Division of Education of the Russell Sage Foundation. 20 pp. No charge.

CLEVELAND EDUCATION SURVEY REPORT

The education survey of Cleveland, Ohio, was conducted during 1915 by the Survey Committee of the Cleveland Foundation. The findings are published in a series of 25 cloth-bound monographs, which are listed below. The price of the entire set is $7.00; single volumes are 25 cents, except as noted. They may be secured from the Division of Education of the Russell Sage Foundation, New York.

Child Accounting in the Public Schools—Ayres.
Educational Extension—Perry.
Education through Recreation—Johnson.
Financing the Public Schools—Clark.
Health Work in the Public Schools—Ayres.
Household Arts and School Lunches—Boughton.
Measuring the Work of the Public Schools—Judd.   50 cts.
Overcrowded Schools and the Platoon Plan—Hartwell.
School Buildings and Equipment—Ayres.
Schools and Classes for Exceptional Children—Mitchell.
School Organization and Administration—Ayres.
The Public Library and the Public Schools—Ayres and
    McKinnie.
The School and the Immigrant—Miller.
The Teaching Staff—Jessup.
What the Schools Teach and Might Teach—Bobbitt.
The Cleveland School Survey (Summary)—Ayres.   50 cts.

Boys and Girls in Commercial Work—Stevens.
Department Store Occupations—O'Leary.
Dressmaking and Millinery—Bryner.
Railroad and Street Transportation—Fleming.
The Building Trades—Shaw.
The Garment Trades—Bryner.
The Metal Trades—Lutz.
The Printing Trades—Shaw.
Wage Earning and Education (Summary)—Lutz.   50 cts.

Printed in the United States
205163BV00001B/361/A

9 780548 761823